HEREFORDSHIRE FROM THE AIR

By Derek Foxton

Published by
Derek Foxton
4 Helensdale Close
Venns Lane
Hereford
HR1 1DP
Telephone 01432 357315
Fax 01432 350555

ISBN 0 9514081-4-3

Printed by
The Amadeus Press
Cleckheaton
West Yorkshire
BD19 4TQ

INTRODUCTION & ACKNOWLEDGMENTS

This book is the result of many flights I took with Bob Bowden from Shobdon Air Field, Herefordshire. All the Hereford City photographs were taken over a period of ten years from helicopters supplied by Mike Davies Air - Services of Rotherwas. I owe a big thank you to both of the above because without their generous help this book would not have been possible.

I took the photographs on high-speed 35mm.film, using Canon EOS cameras, and mostly through curved, scratched Perspex windows which do unfortunately affect the sharpness of the pictures. The weather was often far from ideal as when for example we flew over Belmont Abbey during a spring snow squall.

I designed and arranged the book on my unreliable computer system which my computer engineer Graham Robertson, of Computer Solutions, Hereford, repaired on many occasions at very short notice. The final proof was produced on a new Tiny Computer.

I would like to thank Jean O'Donnell, Mr. & Mrs. Bob Bowden, Basil Butcher, Dominique Foxton, Jessica Foxton and my wife Maria for reading the manuscript and for their help and advice. Also to the following [in no particular order]- Dr. Joan Marsden,Dr Richard Miller, Rob Lloyd from BT Madley, David Whitehead, Ron Shoesmith, Catherine Beal, Eric Turton, Gordon Wood, Arthur & Heather Jason, Anthea Bryan, Alison Fenton, Andrew Foley, Janet Harrison & Pauline Mayglothling at Cadburys, George Kemp, Graham Bateman, The Principals at The Herefordshire Colleges, Ivor Saunders, Gareth Randall, Ian Standing, Michael Raven for allowing me to quote from his book on Herefordshire and finally the staff at The Amadeus Press for all their help and advice.

SELECT BIBLIOGRAPHY

Bridges on the River Wye – Alan Crow.
The Story of Herefordshire's Hospitals – Charles Renton.
The Story of Ross – Hughes & Hurley.
Castles and Moated Sites of Herefordshire – Shoesmith.
A Guide to Herefordshire – Raven.
Herefordshire [The Buildings of England series] – Pevsner.
Herefordshire Vols. 1,2,3. — Royal Commission on Historical Monuments.
Hereford Civic Trust Newsletters.
The Place Names of Herefordshire – Bannister.
A History of the Mansions and Manors of Herefordshire — Robinson.

A History of the Castles of Herefordshire and their Lords – Robinson.
Dinmore Manor – Hollings-Murray.
Eastnor Castle – Hervey-Bathurst.
Berrington Hall – The National Trust.
Croft Castle – The National Trust.
Burkes and Savillls Guide to Country Houses-Herefordshire etc. – Reid.
The Hay and Kington Railways – Rattenbury & Cook.
Belmont Abbey – Anon.
The Book of Hay – Clarke.
Colwall Collection – Ballard.

Robert Symonds, High Sheriff of Herefordshire in the 1600s owned an extensive estate here and the name means his *gate or gap*. The Symonds Yat Rock viewpoint is a major visitor attraction and people come from far and wide to see the spectacular views over the river Wye into Herefordshire. The wood in the foreground is on Huntsham Hill, 500 feet high that rises to the Yat Rock. During the spring the viewpoint is a favourite place for bird watchers who come to look at the nesting peregrine falcons on the nearby cliff face. The river Wye creates a 4-mile long loop around Huntsham Hill and comes back to itself below the Yat Rock only about 1/4 mile from where it began. The only road bridge across the river is the Huntsham Bridge built in 1892 to replace a ferry crossing. Below Symonds Yat is an old railway tunnel, now sealed up, through which ran the line between Monmouth and Chepstow. Some of the old track is now used as a footpath that takes walkers into the Forest of Dean.

SYMONDS YAT

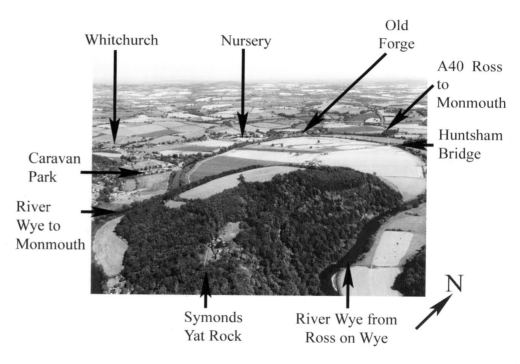

Whitchurch   Nursery   Old Forge   A40 Ross to Monmouth   Huntsham Bridge   Caravan Park   River Wye to Monmouth   Symonds Yat Rock   River Wye from Ross on Wye   N

GOODRICH CASTLE

The name Goodrich means *Godric's* Castle which stands in the south of the county 4 miles southwest of Ross on Wye on a high ridge above the River Wye. Goodrich Castle is the most spectacular medieval castle in the County and from the air it is a landmark seen from miles away and from the ground an impressive sight. The castle overlooks an ancient ford, which was crossed by the Roman Road from Gloucester to Monmouth and Caerleon. The oldest part of the existing castle is the keep that dates from the mid-12th century. By the 14th century the castle had been developed to the shape and size we see today with The Great Hall, 60 feet long, providing the main accommodation. In 1646 the Parliamentarian troops, led by Col. John Birch, took the castle with the help of a specially cast cannon 'Roaring Meg', which could fire a shell of over two hundredweight. 'Roaring Meg' is now on display in the grounds of Churchill House Museum, Hereford. In 1647 Parliament ordered that the lead roof should be removed and so the castle was left to slowly decay. It now belongs to English Heritage. The chapel has recently had a stained glass window commissioned and built. The author's photograph of the castle shows previously unseen extensive crop marks of rectangular shapes to the left of the picture.

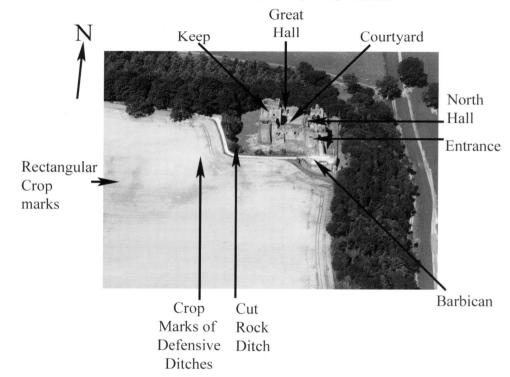

PEMBRIDGE CASTLE

Pembridge Castle is located 1mile northwest of Welsh Newton and 14 miles south of Hereford with the Monmouthshire border only a short distance away. The castle, which is 45 yards long by 30 yards wide, dates from late Norman times and stands on a hillside with wide ranging views to the Black Mountains and Hay Bluff. It was besieged during the Civil War in 1644 and badly damaged. Shoesmith describes it as *a fortified house developed from a 13th century castle and owned by the Pembridge family in 1208 who lost their land in Pembridge to Roger de Mortimer of Wigmore.* In the northern corner of the courtyard there is a chapel that dates back to the 13th century. After the war George Kemble made it his home and at that time St. John Kemble [who was executed in Hereford for his faith in 1679 and buried in Welsh Newton church graveyard] had an oratory in the house. The castle slowly decayed and crumbled over the years but was extensively restored in the early 20th century and is now occupied. It is not open to the public but can be seen from the gate on the C1239 Broad Oak to Welsh Newton road.

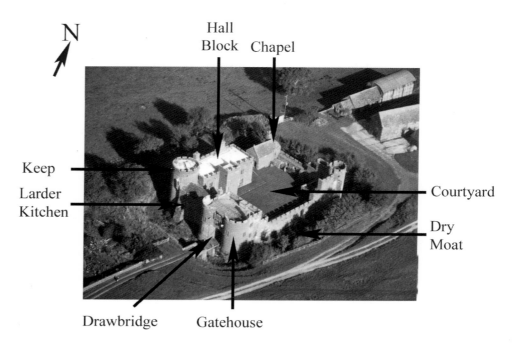

8

Treago castle is situated in a hollow just outside the village of St. Weonards about 9 miles south of Hereford. Sir Richard Mynors is the present owner; the Mynors family have lived here since the early 15th century, this being one of the longest tenures in the County. The building is a fortified house of stone, rectangular with a tower at each corner and has a basement, two floors and an attic. The courtyard has been roofed over and is now an integral part of the house where there is the main staircase and Sir Richard's pipe organ. There were many alterations during the 17th & 18th centuries the most interesting being the projecting smoking room on the upper storey of the southeast tower c1770. The earliest references to the castle are from the 13th century. The sash windows were added in Georgian times.

TREAGO CASTLE

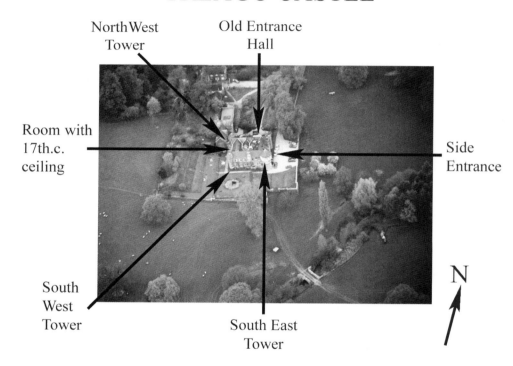

North West Tower

Old Entrance Hall

Room with 17th.c. ceiling

Side Entrance

South West Tower

South East Tower

N

ROSS ON WYE

The name Ross is from the name *rhos,* Welsh for moor or peninsular. The earliest settlers were the Anglo Saxons who lived in Ross and Wilton. The parish church of St. Mary's, which dates from the 12th century, but is mainly of the 13th and 14th centuries and extensively restored in 1734 and 1862, gives the town a picturesque view from the River. Opposite the entrance to the church is the Plague Cross. In the centre of town, at the junction of Broad Street, High Street and Gloucester Road is the Old Market Hall, built in 1651 from local red sandstone. It has two rows of seven columns and arches, while on the wall is a medallion of Charles I. Today it is a heritage centre. The Old Rope Walk is a reminder of an earlier industry when hemp was made into rope. Ross had a distinguished resident, John Kyrle 1637-1724, a local benefactor who gave the citizens of Ross the Prospect Gardens next to the church and the causeway. The castellated tower, known as 'The Gazebo', was formerly called Collins Tower in the 1830s. The town once had a railway station and junction with lines to Hereford, Gloucester and Monmouth that closed in 1964. The Bridstow A40 Bridge was designed by Scott Wilson Kirkpatrick and Partners and built by Tarmac Engineering Ltd in 1960. It has three arches and two piers. The main span is 70 metres with a pavement on each side of the road. The Wye Valley Walk passes under the bridge.

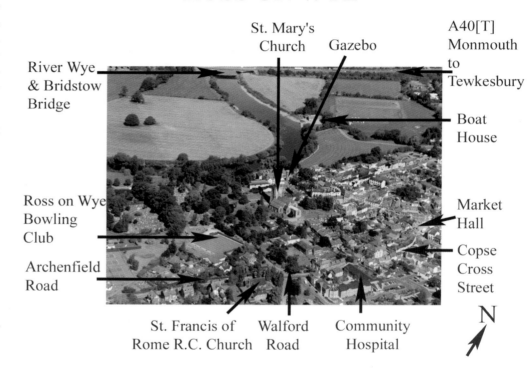

St. Mary's Church   Gazebo   A40[T] Monmouth to Tewkesbury

River Wye & Bridstow Bridge

Boat House

Ross on Wye Bowling Club

Market Hall

Archenfield Road

Copse Cross Street

St. Francis of Rome R.C. Church   Walford Road   Community Hospital

N

Wilton means *settlement of Willa.* The castle stands on raised ground about 70 yards from the River Wye, a site of strategic importance since it guarded the river crossing. There has been a castle here since Norman times but these remains date from the late 13th to early 14th centuries. In the 16th century a house was added to the southwest tower. During the Civil War the castle, then owned by Sir John Brydges, was burnt down and an arch on the north side of the bridge blown up. The present house and ruins have been described as an architectural jungle. The old Wilton Bridge, with its six arches, built about 1600 was the main road link to the west until the opening of the Ross Spur in 1960. It was the second stone bridge to be built across the River Wye and has survived the severe floods of 1795, which destroyed many bridges up stream. In 1914 the bridge was in such a poor state of repair that the river could be seen through the road surface. In 1939 it was widened and strengthened with steel as a wartime measure. There is a sundial in the centre refuge on the downstream side dated 1718. The faces are corroded but a recent time test did suggest that it was 13 minutes slow against G.M.T!

WILTON CASTLE

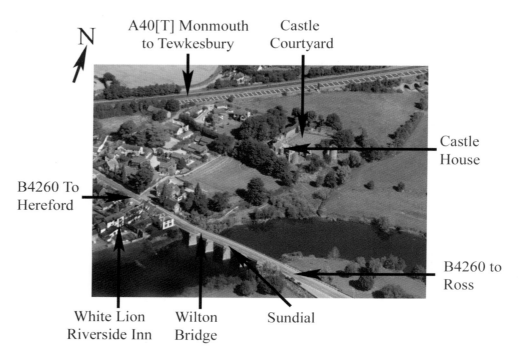

N

A40[T] Monmouth to Tewkesbury

Castle Courtyard

Castle House

B4260 To Hereford

B4260 to Ross

White Lion Riverside Inn

Wilton Bridge

Sundial

Kentchurch Court is the ancient home of the Scudamore family, built in the 14th century as a castle. Part of this survives in the house that was re-built by architect John Nash in the early 19th century. The high tower with the round stone turret dominates the court. Inside are some amazing woodcarvings attributed to the master of the art, Grinling Gibbons. These came from the old Scudamore home at Holme Lacy House [page 30], which were removed when the Earl of Chesterfield sold the house in 1910. The carvings are of garlands with birds, fruit, vegetables etc. The estate still has its deer park, one of very few left from the thirty-five that used to be in the county. The house and estate are only open to the public by appointment.

KENTCHURCH COURT

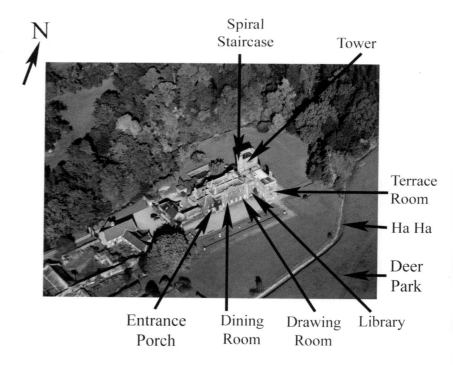

MUCH DEWCHURCH

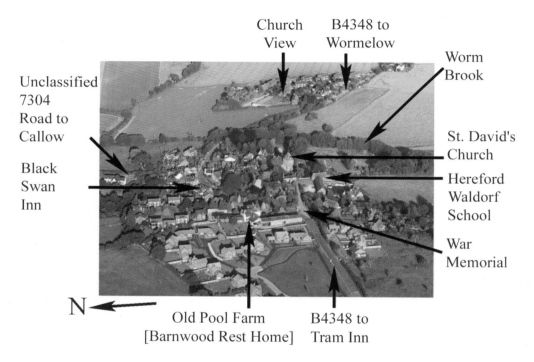

Church View

B4348 to Wormelow

Worm Brook

Unclassified 7304 Road to Callow

St. David's Church

Black Swan Inn

Hereford Waldorf School

War Memorial

N

Old Pool Farm [Barnwood Rest Home]

B4348 to Tram Inn

The name Much Dewchurch means *the church of Dewi,* old Welsh for David. The Welsh language was spoken here until the middle of the 17th century. The village developed round the parish church of St. David, which is Norman with a 13th century tower. Inside it has monuments to the Pye family from the nearby Mynde House, which lies about 1 1/4 miles south west of the church. This photograph shows relatively new houses that have created a 20th century dormitory village for Hereford. On close examination some earlier build-

ings and the school can be seen. The village inn, The Black Swan, dates from the 15th century and has some internal period features including a stone spiral staircase. The old vicarage is Elizabethan and was once the village school. Low banks some 300 yards to the north east of the church cover the remains of a motte and bailey castle and it is likely that there are stone remains below the surface.

MUCH BIRCH

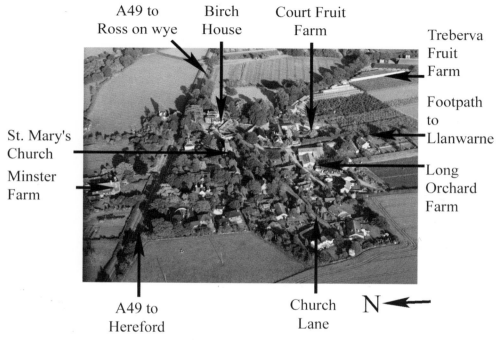

A49 to Ross on wye · Birch House · Court Fruit Farm · Treberva Fruit Farm · Footpath to Llanwarne · St. Mary's Church · Minster Farm · Long Orchard Farm · A49 to Hereford · Church Lane · N

The village centre is concentrated near the parish church of St. Mary and St. Thomas of Canterbury that was entirely re-built in 1837 by Thomas Foster retaining only some fittings from the original building. Nicholas Pevsner describes it as *all eaves on corbels, and the west tower, a typical feature of the date, with battlements on corbels*. There is a painting on the chancel ceiling of cherubs' heads in the sky peeping over little clouds and the stained glass windows are described as high Victorian. The village inn, The Axe and Cleaver, which is 3/4 mile away, is a 17th century building at the southeastern end of the village and over one mile along the A49 to the north west is the Pilgrim Hotel. On the C1263 road to Kingsthorne is a new monastery built by the nuns of Poor Clares who moved out of their convent in Lower Bullingham near Hereford in 1996. The old monastery had become surrounded by new housing estates that intruded into their privacy, so they sold the buildings and land for development and built on a new site near the primary school where they have a panoramic view of the Welsh Mountains.

BRYNGWYN

Bryngwyn House is situated near to Wormelow Tump 6 miles south of Hereford. The name is Welsh meaning *white hill*. The house was designed by the Hereford architect F.R. Kempson and his colleague Martin in 1868 for Sir James Reginald Rankin M.P., a local benefactor, who donated a substantial sum of money to pay eighty per cent of the building costs of the Hereford Free Library in Broad Street. He also founded the Hereford County College – now the Royal National College for the Blind. In late Victorian times, Bryngwyn was extended and a larger drawing room, ballroom, conservatory and billiard room were added. There was an earlier moated house, about 400 yards to the northwest which in 1681 was the scene of a murder. Robert Pye, of the nearby estate The Mynde, was a Protestant magistrate who attempted to serve a summons on his Catholic neighbour at Bryngwyn where a struggle took place and Robert Pye was killed. In 1915, the estate of 2,938 acres, which included twenty-two farms that brought in an income of £3,555 a year, was sold at auction. There is a story that in the early 1930's Mr Oakley, a dentist, went to an auction to bid for a part of the big house but later discovered that his bid had bought the whole house and surrounding grounds. He later converted it to a hotel, which was advertised as first class with forty bedrooms, every modern convenience and a ballroom that could hold 200 dancers. There were 20 acres of parkland and 60 of woodland. Pevsner describes the house as *Tudor, stone, gabled with an asymmetrical front but all the same like a school or an institution*. Today the house is used as an engineering workshop and flats.

Old
Bakehouse
Larder
Diary
Coalhouse
Bootroom

Timothy
Ormerod
Engineering

"New
Wing"

N

Old Hall   Old Study
Staircase
Entrance Hall

The Madley Communications Centre, previously known as the Satellite Earth Station, is one of the major links this country has with the outside world. The large dishes are a substantial landmark, visible from many miles away. This site was one of the busiest airfields during the last war with flights around the clock. It was also used for training wireless operators for operational squadrons. It opened in August 1941 with 60 Proctor and 18 Dominie aeroplanes and trained 2,800 ground and 1,200 aircrew wireless operators who used bicycles to get around the large area. It was not a favourite place for pilots due to a combination of hilly country on three sides and almost instant weather changes. Rudolph Hess was flown out of this base to his war trial in Germany. Until 1978 the country only had one satellite earth station, that at Goonhilly Downs in Cornwall, so it was decided that, with a predicted growth in satellite communications, a new site was required. Madley was chosen *because of the low radio interference, good foundations and geographically convenient,* so the Post Office [now B.T.] purchased Street House Farm of 140 acres at £1,000 per acre. By 1980 several dishes had been built at a cost of £12 million, the largest being 120 feet high and 105 feet in diameter. These are in contact with satellites over the Atlantic and Indian areas. Today the electronics have gone far into the digital age and Madley provides uplinks for many T.V. services. Nowadays other specialist work is carried out and Madley provides expert assistance to developing countries and provides staff for lucrative contracts to provide satellite ground stations in the third world and former eastern block countries. The use of satellites for T.V. will always be favoured because of their flexibility and remote access capability. The future of Madley, as probably the largest single communications centre in the world, is thus assured.

MADLEY
COMMUNICATIONS CENTRE

Switching Centre

Administration Building

Indian Ocean Dish 32m. diameter

Atlantic Ocean Dish 32m. diameter

N

The name Olchon was first mentioned in 1130 and spelt *elchon* meaning *brook*. The Olchon Brook runs along the floor of the valley, which lies at the extreme south west of the County with the English, Welsh and Herefordshire common boundary running along the top of the Black Mountains above the valley. This is also the route of Offa's Dyke long distance footpath. Just over the mountain is the Vale of Ewyas with Llanthony Priory and the village of Capel-y-ffin. To the left of the picture is the high ridge of Black Hill with the Golden Valley and Peterchurch in the far distance. In the 17th century the area had a few large farms with large herds of cattle, then in the 18th and 19th centuries a number of smallholdings were created and flocks of sheep were introduced. Gaps in the windswept hedges can be seen but the original field patterns remain. This valley was the site of several Bronze Age burials that were found during ploughing. St. Thomas Well, a spring in a field on private property near SO 284321 is one of the many healing wells found in Herefordshire and is said to help rheumatism and weak eyes. Because of its exceptional purity the water is used in Bach's Flower Remedies.

OLCHON VALLEY

Black Hill

Golden Valley

Cae Thomas Well [Spring]

Town House

N

Olchon Brook

Olchon Valley Road

CLODOCK

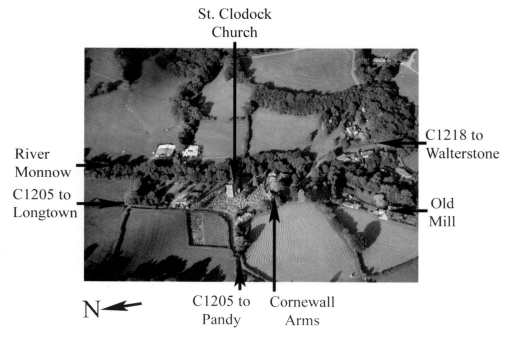

St. Clodock
Church

River
Monnow

C1205 to
Longtown

C1218 to
Walterstone

Old
Mill

N ←

C1205 to
Pandy

Cornewall
Arms

The name Clodock, comes from *St. Clydawg*. The legend tells that Prince Clydawg, son of King Cledwyn, a 5th century King of Ewias, was out hunting one day when a rival in love murdered him. His body was removed for burial on a cart pulled by two oxen but they refused to cross the Monnow at the ford and then the yoke broke. These were taken to be signs that the prince should be buried here. He had led a godly life and because of his murder was made a martyr. He was sanctified, pilgrims came to visit his tomb, and a church was built, first in timber and then in stone. The church has a long Norman nave and a late medieval tower. Evidence of the early 9th century church has survived in a memorial stone behind the pulpit with the sad inscription, *to the faithful and dear wife of Guinndas, native of this place.* On the River Monnow stands a corn mill that has a large water wheel made at Leominster in 1848. The Offa's Dyke long distance footpath runs along the adjacent high mountain ridge which is also the Welsh and Herefordshire County boundary. The C1205 road passes the church and cemetery.

HOLME LACY HOUSE

Holme Lacy House lies about 4 miles south east of Hereford on the C1266 road situated on a spur of higher ground looking across the river Wye Valley. The Scudamore family purchased the estate in 1354 and Charles I stayed here during the Civil War. The present house was built about 1673 when it was no more than one room deep at any point and access to each room was through the previous one. The last of the Scudamore owners was the Earl of Chesterfield who sold it in 1910. The external style is Palladian and the layout was in the shape of the letter H. Sir Lucas Tooth, who purchased the house in 1911, added the ballroom and the present staircase. Inside the house, the very ornate ceilings in eight of the rooms have survived from the original building. They are said to be the finest of their period in this Country. There are many original fittings but sadly most of the Grinling Gibbon's woodcarvings have been either sold or taken to Kentchurch Court [page 16], the present Scudamore home. The last owners to use it as a home, were the Wills family of tobacco fame, and on the death of Mr. Wills, his wife presented the house to Herefordshire Council who converted it into a hospital for ladies. It was sold in 1981 and has since had several owners but now Warner Holidays have a long lease. They have extended and converted it into a 181-bedroom hotel with health spa, several dining rooms and an entertainment centre. It is reputed to have a friendly ghost.

Blue Room · Old Ballroom [now Restaurant] · East Lawn · Dining Room · Sitting Room · Bedrooms · N · Swimming Pool & Health Spa · Pavilion Concert Hall

FOWNHOPE

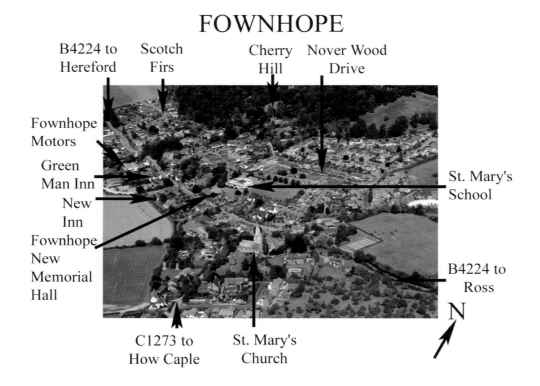

B4224 to Hereford · Scotch Firs · Cherry Hill · Nover Wood Drive · Fownhope Motors · Green Man Inn · New Inn · Fownhope New Memorial Hall · St. Mary's School · B4224 to Ross · C1273 to How Caple · St. Mary's Church · N

The name Fownhope is an interesting one. In 1242 it was *Fagehope* meaning *fawn* and *hope valley*. It is situated almost half way between Hereford and Ross on Wye on the B4224 road and is a thriving village with recent expansion north west of the church. The parish church of St. Mary has a Norman tower with a 14th century shingle-covered spire. Inside is a well-preserved Norman tympanum. The village stocks are still to be found outside the church.

The wooded lower slopes of Cherry Hill are on the upper left of the picture. On the hilltop is an overgrown Iron Age Fort. The village has a modern Village Hall, several shops, a large garage with a Mitsubishi main agency and one of Herefordshire's most famous village inns, The Green Man, which is a timber-framed building with a modern leisure complex in the grounds. The Inn was at one time a courthouse for Petty Sessions.

MADLEY

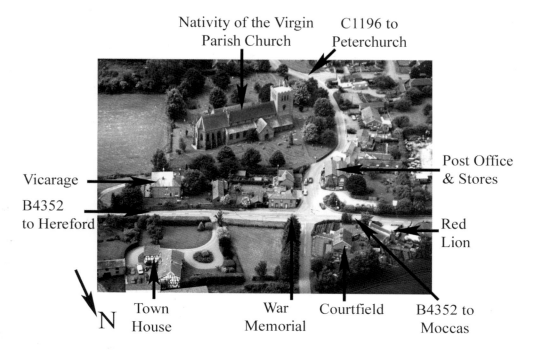

Nativity of the Virgin Parish Church

C1196 to Peterchurch

Post Office & Stores

Vicarage

B4352 to Hereford

Red Lion

N

Town House

War Memorial

Courtfield

B4352 to Moccas

Madley, named from the Old Welsh matle, *good place,* lies 7 miles south west of Hereford and south of the river Wye. The castle, which is about 1/4 mile north of the church, has a few remains of the motte and bailey but they are in poor condition having been badly damaged about 60 years ago. The parish church of St. Mary, which dates from the 12th century, is in the centre of the village near the crossroads and has a crypt under the east end of the 14th century chancel. Inside, the church is unusually large and has a substantial tower and some early stained glass from the 13th century. The old churchyard cross still survives though its head is badly weathered. The Madley Music Festival is held in the church every year during July. The Memorial Cross has been recently moved to the north east corner of the junction. The village shop is opposite the church and the Red Lion Inn is nearby.

MORDIFORD

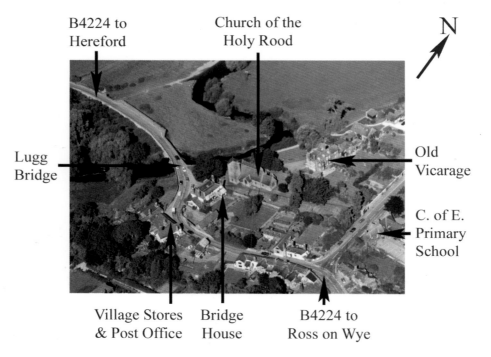

B4224 to Hereford

Church of the Holy Rood

N

Lugg Bridge

Old Vicarage

C. of E. Primary School

Village Stores & Post Office

Bridge House

B4224 to Ross on Wye

The village of Mordiford, or Mawr-ty-ford in Welsh, meaning *great house by a ford* lies 4 miles east of Hereford. The bridge over the River Lugg was the site of a minor Civil War battle that was defended by Barnabas Scudamore. It has nine arches but only two span the river; the pointed westernmost arch was built in the 14th century while the other arches are rounded and of the 16th century. The River Lugg was once navigable with locks for small barges as far as Leominster. The parish church of the Holy Rood, which stands on the east bank of the River Lugg has a Norman arched doorway but was extensively rebuilt with a central tower and spire in the early 19th century. On the west wall of the church there was a painting illustrating "The Tale of The Mordiford Dragon". The village has a primary school, a public house called the Moon Inn, and a shop and Post Office. Nearby is the 'Spout', a natural spring accessible to the public.

WOOLHOPE

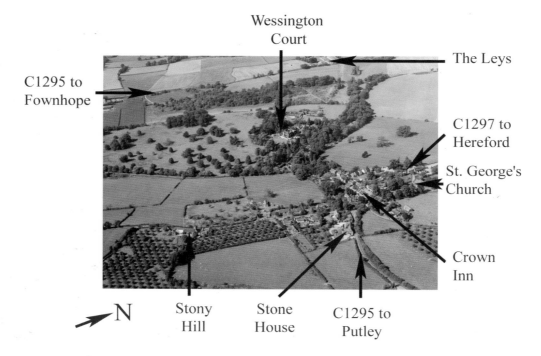

Wessington Court

The Leys

C1295 to Fownhope

C1297 to Hereford

St. George's Church

Crown Inn

N

Stony Hill

Stone House

C1295 to Putley

The name Woolhope means *Wulfgifu's valley*. Wulfgifu and her sister Lady Godiva, donated their manor to Hereford Cathedral in the 11th century, before the Norman Conquest. Woolhope is situated 7 miles south east of Hereford on the Woolhope Dome, which is a Silurian Limestone formation. The Crown Inn, noted for its generous helpings of food, is adjacent to the churchyard. The parish church of St. George is Norman with 13th century additions and inside there are several interesting coffin lids of this period. There is a 14th century cross in the graveyard approached through a 17th century lych gate. Wessington Court is one of the largest houses in the parish, built in the Tudor style during the 1890's for H. W. Booth with a great oak staircase behind a screen. It has magnificent views towards Gloucestershire and the Forest of Dean. The Herefordshire Nature Trust manages several fields and woods near the house and is implementing a tree-planting scheme.

LEDBURY

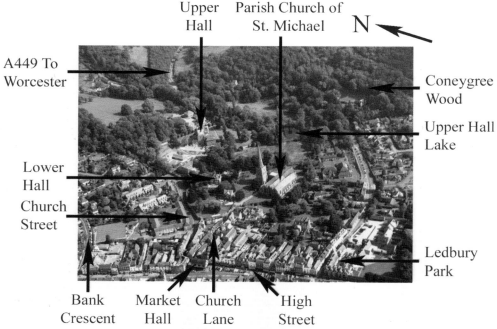

Upper Hall

Parish Church of St. Michael

N

A449 To Worcester

Coneygree Wood

Upper Hall Lake

Lower Hall Church Street

Bank Crescent

Market Hall

Church Lane

High Street

Ledbury Park

The name Ledbury means the *hill or mound by the river Leadon*. The town is well known for its picturesque timber-framed Market Hall and Church Lane. In many buildings, behind the brick facades are some excellent examples of timber-frame work and early wall paintings, some of which can be seen in the Council building in Church Street. The Market Hall, built in 1617 by John Abel, has a distinctive herringbone pattern. The lofty parish church of Saint Michael, founded in 720, has a detached bell tower with eight bells. Near the church are Upper Hall and Lower Hall [with a swimming pool in the garden]. Upper Hall was home to the Martin family [who owned Martins Bank] until 1923 when it was sold and opened as the Grammar School. In 1991 the buildings, then used as the John Masefield Junior School, closed and moved to the Mabels Furlong site. It is now immaculately restored and converted into several apartments retaining the original fixtures and fittings. The landscaped grounds of Upper Hall have been restored and are closed to the public. Lay Vicars once owned both these houses and lived on a portion of the income from the Ledbury Churches. Nicholas Pevsner describes the Barrett Browning Memorial Institute and Clock Tower [opposite the Market Hall], built in 1896, as *really terrible*. Ledbury Park is a fine black and white house at the junction of the Worcester road and Upper Cross. It was built by the Biddulph family in 1600 and described as the grandest black and white house in the county. The house is now converted into several apartments that retain the original features.

LEDBURY
RAILWAY VIADUCT

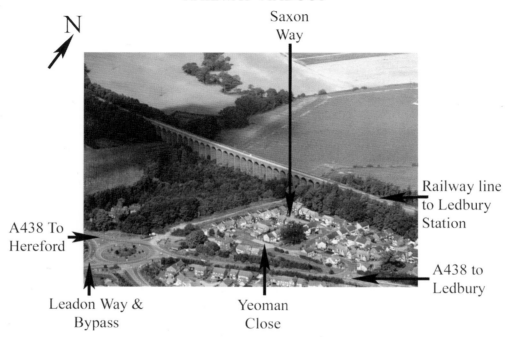

Saxon Way

N

Railway line to Ledbury Station

A438 To Hereford

A438 to Ledbury

Leadon Way & Bypass

Yeoman Close

The railway line from Hereford to Worcester was the last of the major lines built into Hereford. The chosen route presented the engineers with several major obstacles, the largest being the Malvern Hills and Ledbury tunnels. The Ledbury tunnel was a very poor design, which during construction had rock falls, water penetration and poor ventilation and was said to be the most foul tunnel in the Country. The viaduct had to be erected to keep the line level with the nearby Ledbury tunnel and to cross the River Leadon valley. It has thirty-one arches, is 330 yards long, more than 60 feet high and was built using more than 5 million bricks, all made on site using portable kilns and local clay by three hundred women from Staffordshire, who carried the clay on their heads to the brick kilns. When the viaduct was built a small railway at ground level was used to move materials and help with construction. The main engineers were Sir Morton Peto and Steven Ballard of Colwall. Ballard was the engineer in charge of the construction of the canal from Hereford to Ledbury in 1845. The line to Hereford opened in September 1861, and this led to the slow downfall of the Hereford to Gloucester Canal, which virtually closed in 1880 when the route from Ledbury to Gloucester was replaced by the railway. The railway line is now a single track from Malvern Wells to Hereford.

EASTNOR CASTLE

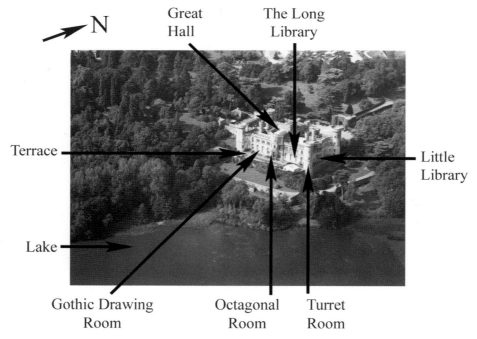

Eastnor Castle, on the eastern edge of Herefordshire and at the southern end of the Malvern Hills was built for the first Earl Somers between 1810 and 1824, possibly as a display of his wealth and social standing. He employed the architect Robert Smirke to design the castle to create the impression of an Edward I fortress guarding the Welsh borders. The 4,000 tons of stone came from the Forest of Dean and arrived in Ledbury by canal. The castle cost £85,923 [approximately £8.5 million today] to build. It was never completely finished due to a shortage of funds, as an orangery was proposed but never built. The castle measures 320 feet by 180 feet with a 60 feet high entrance hall. The Gothic Dining Room, designed by A.W. Pugin for the second Earl in 1849 has a huge chimneypiece with the family tree on it, and the whole room is full of furniture designed by Pugin. The octagonal room, with its view over the lake, has a new carpet specially woven in China. The long library was designed for the 3rd Earl with shelving made in Italy and has 17th century Flemish tapestries hanging above. The little library has been restored and is now a billiard room. The Great Hall in the middle of the building is 60 feet long and 55 feet high and is where the armour collection was displayed until 1989. The castle and grounds are open to the public in the summer with regular events throughout the year.

The Malvern Hills form the eastern boundary of the county of Herefordshire and the highest summit of the range in the county is the Herefordshire Beacon. The Beacon is an Iron Age hill fort built on the southern end of the hills that covers an area of 32 acres, and is irregular in shape with a massive inner rampart and ditch which follows the contour line. Excavations undertaken in the late 1870s and a century later by S. C. Stanford, revealed finds that varied from flint stones to Romano - British pottery and pottery from the 12th century. A few ancient stones mark the county boundary. The whole area is open to the public and has a footpath, the Worcester Way, passing through.

HEREFORDSHIRE BEACON

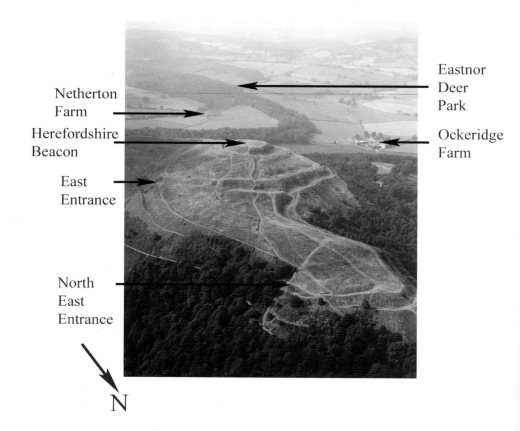

Netherton Farm

Herefordshire Beacon

East Entrance

North East Entrance

Eastnor Deer Park

Ockeridge Farm

N

COLWALL

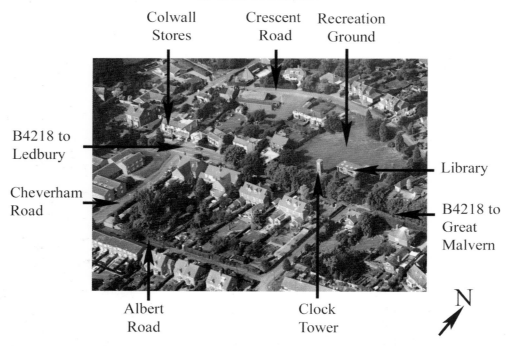

Colwall Stores   Crescent Road   Recreation Ground

B4218 to Ledbury

Cheverham Road

Library

B4218 to Great Malvern

Albert Road

Clock Tower

N

Colwall is named in the Domesday Book as *colewelle* meaning *cool well or spring*. Malvern water is possibly the best-known English spring water and is used by Royalty. In the past there were several bottling plants on both sides of the Malvern Hills but the only one left in the village is now owned by Coca-Cola-Schweppes. Their water is piped from Primes Well that in ancient times, together with Waums Well, supplied the Herefordshire Beacon and Iron Age hillfort. The Worcester to Hereford Railway [just off the lower edge of the picture] first arrived in 1851 following the construction of the tunnel through the Malvern Hills. Colwall Stone is the modern heart of Colwall

that developed in late Victorian times after the arrival of the Railway. Colwall Stone, according to the legend, is a limestone block rolled down the hill by a giant to bring his unfaithful wife and her lover to a sticky end. Tom Pedlingham erected the Clock Tower in 1931. To the right is the Humphrey Walwyn Library built in 1957 by the Walwyn Education Foundation. It was presented to the village in 1992, is owned by the Parish Council and still used as a village library run by Herefordshire Council. Colwall Stores and the butcher's shop are to the left.

BELMONT ABBEY

Herefordshire Community Health Trust

Hedley Lodge

C1199 to Hereford →

Monastry

C1199 to Eaton Bishop

St. Michael's Abbey

N

Belmont Abbey meaning *beautiful hill* in French was designed by Pugin & Pugin, successors to the well-known A.W.N. Pugin. The work was commissioned by Mr Wegg-Prosser of Belmont House in 1854 and completed in 1859. It became the Catholic Cathedral for the newly established diocese of Newport and the seat of its bishop until 1920 after which it became a Benedictine Abbey. The oldest part of the church is the nave that is faced in Bath stone. Pevsner describes the other buildings that make up the monastery *as rather depressingly institutional Gothic*. The Monks opened a boarding school in 1917 that could accommodate up to 200 boys. The Headmaster and House Masters were monks who were supported by lay staff that maintained the high standards expected of a traditional English Benedictine School. Sadly it had to close in the mid 1990's due to falling pupil numbers and the buildings are now occupied by the Herefordshire Community Health Trust. The Abbey runs a very successful guesthouse, Hedley Lodge, which provides accommodation for visitors and caters for functions. There is also a printing workshop run by the monks.

BARTESTREE CONVENT
& St. MICHAEL'S HOSPICE

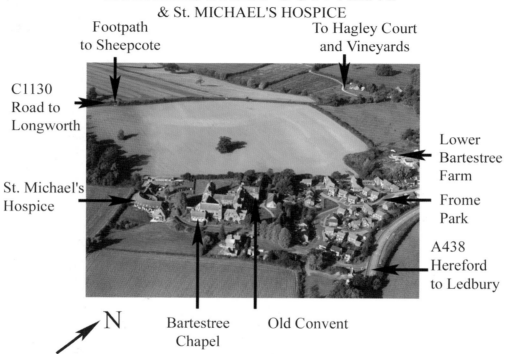

Footpath to Sheepcote

To Hagley Court and Vineyards

C1130 Road to Longworth

Lower Bartestree Farm

St. Michael's Hospice

Frome Park

A438 Hereford to Ledbury

N

Bartestree Chapel

Old Convent

Bartestree, named after *Beortwealds Tree,* lies on the A438 Hereford to Ledbury Road. This picture shows the old Bartestree Convent and St. Michael's Hospice. The Convent of Our Lady of Charity and Refuge was built in 1863 on land donated by Robert Biddulph Phillips of Longworth Hall to designs by Edwin Welby Pugin. The Convent provided a refuge for 'fallen women' who were employed in the making of underwear and in the commercial laundry run by the nuns until its closure in 1975. By the time the convent closed, the nuns were driving cars, watching T.V., playing tennis as well as doing their usual tapestry work. The Convent sadly had to close after a business venture collapsed and it was recently sold for £250,000. The Nuns had their own private chapel and in 1870 a 14th century chapel from a site near Longworth Hall was moved and rebuilt in the Convent grounds for public services.

A local lady - Freda Pearce initiated a massive fund raising campaign to build a Hospice here on land leased by the Convent for 99 years at a rent of 5p. per year. The architect was Nigel Dees and built by H. Vaughan & Sons for £750,000 including equipment. Princess Alexandra came to open it in May 1985.

STOKE EDITH

The name Stoke Edith means *the holy place of Queen Edith,* wife of Edward the Confessor, who owned the manor in 1066 when it had two priests and a mill. It is situated 7 miles east of Hereford on the A438 road to Ledbury. Outside the Old Rectory on the roadside is Edith's Well, which is covered by a metal grill installed by Lady Emily Foley about 100 years ago. The parish church of St. Mary has a tower that was built in the 14th century and houses six bells and its thin recessed spire has been shortened and capped. The local landowners, the Foleys, rebuilt most of the church in 1742. Inside is a fine monument to Paul Foley of 1699. Nearby, the Old Rectory is now the home of Andrew Foley who describes the house as cold with thin walls. Behind the church to the east, are the ruins of Stoke Edith Park House that was rebuilt at the end of the 17th century by Thomas Foley who purchased the estate in 1670. The house was burnt down in 1927 and the shell rebuilt in 1936 but this was finally demolished in 1957. The house contained some priceless murals and ceilings that were painted by Sir James Thornhill. Humphrey Repton whose red book survives with the family, landscaped the grounds. In recent years the Old Rectory was a restaurant and small hotel where Andrew Lloyd-Webber and Tim Rice once stayed and wrote much of *Jesus Christ Super Star.*

Remains of West Wing

Site of Stoke Edith House

St. Mary's Church

Old Rectory

N

HEREFORD CATHEDRAL

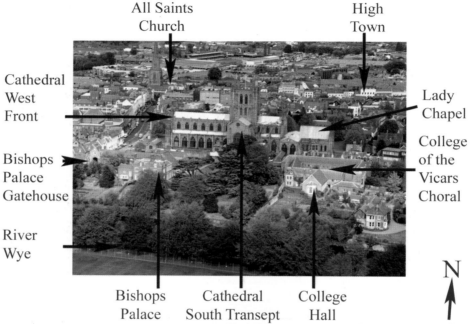

All Saints Church

High Town

Cathedral West Front

Lady Chapel

College of the Vicars Choral

Bishops Palace Gatehouse

River Wye

Bishops Palace

Cathedral South Transept

College Hall

N

Hereford Cathedral, built between 1085-1148 and dedicated by Bishop Robert Bethune, stands on a bank above the River Wye. The Lady Chapel is a fine example of Early English style. The central Norman tower had a lead spire that was removed during rebuilding; a new one of 150 feet was proposed but never built. There was once a West Front Tower that collapsed on Easter Monday 1786. Architect James Wyatt then designed a new, very plain West Front without a tower and also shortened the aisle by one bay. The West Front was rebuilt again between 1904-1908 by Oldrid Scott using stone from Hollington in Staffordshire at a cost of £16,000. Princess Henry of Battenberg unveiled the memorial window to Queen Victoria during her visit in 1902.

The Bishop's Palace was built around a Norman timber-framed hall of about 1180, which is thought to be the oldest secular timberframed building in the country that is still occupied. Some of the original Norman timbers that can still be seen hidden behind doors in the pillars of the Great Hall are 30 inches in diameter. The Vicars Choral was built during the years 1472-1475 to accommodate the singing Vicars. They originally lived at 29 Castle Street where their 14th century hall survives. All Saints Church, which dates from the early 13th century, has the highest spire in the county at 240 feet tall. Most of the buildings on the north side of High Town can be seen in this view.

HEREFORD
CITY CENTRE

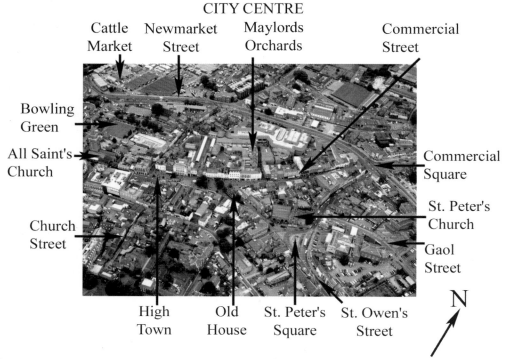

Cattle Market — Newmarket Street — Maylords Orchards — Commercial Street — Bowling Green — All Saint's Church — Commercial Square — St. Peter's Church — Church Street — Gaol Street — High Town — Old House — St. Peter's Square — St. Owen's Street — N

Central Hereford is a rather complex mosaic when seen from the air. From this height the roads look like a map that makes it easier to identify the different streets and buildings. The Inner Relief Road [Newmarket Street] follows the old medieval City Wall that surrounds the city centre and High Town in the middle of the picture. To the north of the Relief Road are the Cattle Market, Garrick House and the multi-storey car park. High Town is an open space with the Old House at the eastern end. The new buildings are the Maylord Orchards Shopping Centre that opened in 1985. The shop fronts of nearly all the buildings on the north side of High Town are visible as well as All Saints Church, St. Peters Church and the major banks. The two green grass squares are the Bowling Green and St.Thomas Cantilupe School's playing field. The roofs of both the Town Hall and the Shire Hall are to the lower right corner.

HEREFORD
CASTLE STREET

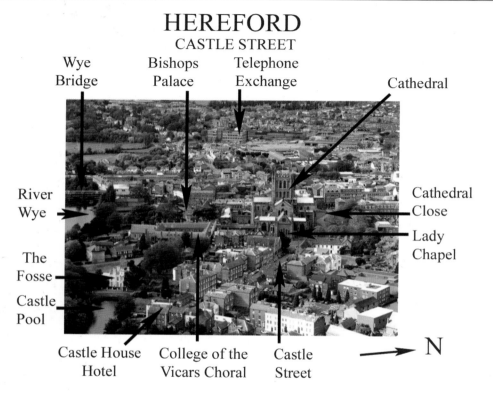

This view shows Castle Street leading to the Cathedral Close. Most of the buildings in Castle Street are Georgian but several have an earlier timber-framed interior. Inside number 29 is a late 14th century hall, originally used by the Vicars Choral and now a part of the Cathedral School. Castle House Hotel, formerly the Castle Pool Hotel, was originally built as a pair of town houses and has recently undergone a full refurbishment by its owners Dr. and Mrs Albert Heijn, offering very luxurious accommodation and high cuisine.

A member of the Bulmer family now owns the Fosse which was designed by architect Robert Smirke [later Sir] who was also architect of the Hereford Shire Hall and later the British Museum. It was built on the site of the old castle moat. The Castle pool now known as the duck pond, is the last remaining part of the moat. Behind the Fosse is the site of the castle motte, which was a very high man-made mound of gravel with a stone keep on top.

High Town has been the centre of the City since Norman times. All Saints Church tower has eight bells that are in regular use and the steeple, at 240 feet high, is the tallest in the County. The church has recently undergone a £1.8 million restoration with a modern, award winning café installed at the west end. St Peter's Church, was first built in 1085 by Walter de-Lacy who fell from the scaffolding and died while inspecting its construction. The present church was built during the early to mid-13th century. The tower contains five bells, but they are not in use at present. The Shire Hall was built on the site of the old county gaol that was demolished about 1805. It was designed by Robert Smirke [later Sir] in 1815 and opened in 1817. Inside there is a large assembly room used for public functions, two Crown Courtrooms (one being the second oldest in England), committee rooms, and the Herefordshire Council Mobile Library Service. The old Police Station, now the Magistrates' Courts, was once part of the old City Gaol before being purchased by the City Council. A new court building is being built in Bath Street near Commercial Square. The Town Hall had its foundation stone laid on May 13th 1902 and was built with a facade of terracotta brick. It served as the Town Hall for the City Council until 1998 when the new Herefordshire Council was formed. The City Mayor has a parlour and a secretary's office here. Maylord Orchards Shopping Centre is on the right and in the distance is the Green Dragon Hotel.

HEREFORD
HIGH TOWN

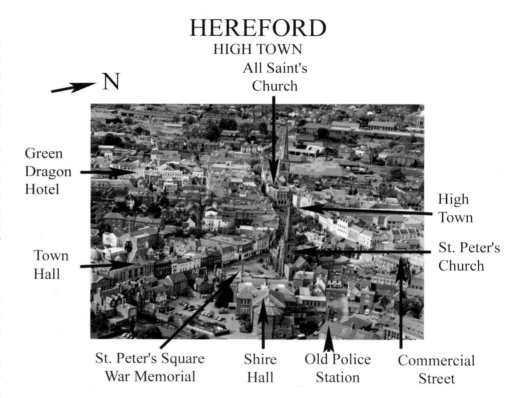

All Saint's Church

N

Green Dragon Hotel

High Town

Town Hall

St. Peter's Church

St. Peter's Square War Memorial

Shire Hall

Old Police Station

Commercial Street

HEREFORD
HINTON

The radiating roads from Hinton Crescent form a distinct pattern. The Hereford City Council built the estate of 391 homes in 1930 and today more than half are privately owned. The Oak Crescent development of Cornish Unit Construction was built in 1946 and Ash Avenue in 1956 as 16 warden assisted homes. The parish church of St. Martins originally stood near the Wye Bridge but was destroyed during the Civil War in 1645 by the Royalist City defenders to remove an advantage point overlooking the Old Wye Bridge from the attacking Parliamentarians. The present church, built at a cost of £5,000, was consecrated and opened on September 30th 1845. Queen Victoria donated £1,000 because of the peculiar circumstances in which the original church was lost. The church bell was exhibited and used at the great International Exhibition of 1862. The chancel was extended in 1895 to commemorate the 50th anniversary. In 1895 part of the spire was blown down and the following year an earthquake removed a further portion so it was later rebuilt.

The Rev. Dr Talbot of Ullingswick founded the General Hospital in 1775. It was built on land donated by the Earl of Oxford, adjacent to the medieval castle site on the banks of the River Wye, and opened in 1783 as the General Infirmary. The original building was extended in 1831 after a bequest of £10,000. The City decided to celebrate Queen Victoria's Jubilee by erecting a children's ward that was opened in 1888. Before the foundation of the National Health Service in 1948, the hospital depended on subscriptions and donations as well as fundraising events. The hospital will close on completion of the new building at the County Hospital site. In the foreground is the King George Playing Field and riverside walk. The Victoria Suspension Bridge was built to commemorate Queen Victoria's Jubilee of 1897. It was designed by the City Surveyor and built at a cost of £1,200 by Corporation workmen and opened by Lady Emily Foley in 1898. In the centre of Castle Green is the Nelson Monument. Nelson was made a Freeman of the City in 1802 during his visit that year. The column was erected in 1809 but, due to lack of funds, the top has an urn instead of a statue.

HEREFORD
GENERAL HOSPITAL

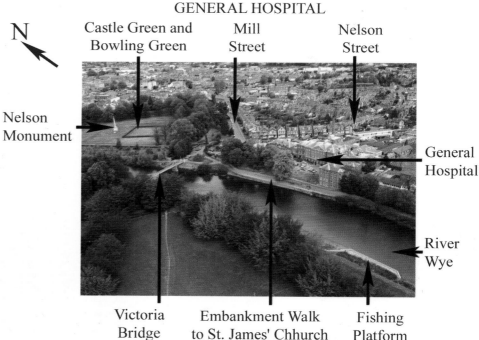

N

Castle Green and Bowling Green

Mill Street

Nelson Street

Nelson Monument

General Hospital

River Wye

Victoria Bridge

Embankment Walk to St. James' Chhurch

Fishing Platform

Hereford's main educational campus, on Aylestone Hill about one mile east of the City centre is the site of Hereford Sixth Form College, Herefordshire College of Technology, and Herefordshire College of Art. Nearby are Aylestone School and Broadlands School. This whole area was the former Broadlands House estate, which in 1915 was advertised for sale with 35 acres of land. The sale brochure had several illustrations of the landscaped gardens as well as the house, which belonged to Judge Harris-Lea. The estate plan indicated that there was an entrance lodge in Folly Lane and a long drive to the house, which is now a part of Aylestone School. In 1962 Herefordshire Technical College moved from Newtown Road into their new buildings, which provided a main office, lecture rooms, an assembly hall and workshops. The School of Farriery continued to use the site at Newtown Road until 1999. The Herefordshire College of Art opened in 1970 and the Sixth Form College was built in 1972 and opened the following year. All the colleges have expanded over the years and the Sixth Form College has recently announced further plans to enlarge the sports department. Several large houses in Folly Lane that are on the photograph have recently been demolished to make way for new houses. The two that are left are Hatterall, Hair, Beauty and Holistic Therapy Centre, and Carfax House, which is used for administration. The student numbers for the year 1999/2000 were as follows:

Herefordshire Technical College –Full time 1385, Part time 8,920, Non- Vocational 3,676. Total 13,981.

Herefordshire College of Art –Further Education 318, Part time 308, Higher Education 169. Total 795.

Hereford Sixth Form College- First year 557, Second year 463. Total 1,020.

HEREFORDSHIRE COLLEGES
AYLESTONE HILL

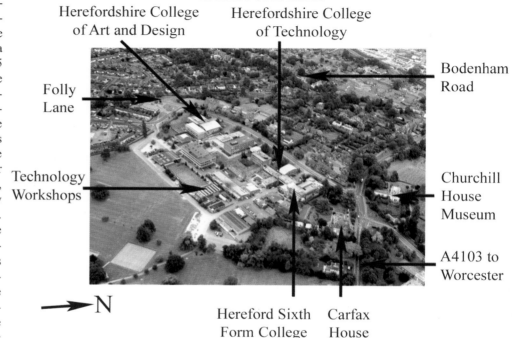

Herefordshire College of Art and Design

Herefordshire College of Technology

Folly Lane

Bodenham Road

Technology Workshops

Churchill House Museum

A4103 to Worcester

N

Hereford Sixth Form College

Carfax House

HEREFORD
ROYAL NATIONAL COLLEGE FOR THE BLIND

St. Francis Xavier's School

R.N.C.B. Main Building

Piano Tuning Dept.

N

Venns Lane

Gardner Building

Queen's Building

College Road

College Green

Penn Grove Road

The campus of the Royal National College for the Blind is situated at the top of College Hill 1 mile northeast of Hereford. It was built by F. R. Kempson in 1880 in the style of the Victorian Gothic revival complete with narrow ecclesiastical windows and a central tower. It opened as 'The County College', a boy's school under the management of a limited company, but was not a success and wound up in 1903 when it was put up for sale. The Hereford Times described it as a white elephant. The Herefordshire Education Committee purchased the buildings in 1904 for £8,500, and so became the first Local Education Authority in the Country to open a Teachers' Training College. It closed in 1977 but reopened in October 1978 as The Royal National College for the Blind, which was founded in 1872, and moved to Hereford from its previous home in Shropshire. There are three halls of residence on the north side of Venns Lane and one on the main campus. Her Majesty The Queen opened the rectangular shaped Queen's Building in 1987.

Brinsop Court lies 6 miles west of Hereford. In the 13th & 14th centuries the house belonged to the family of Tirrell and then passed to the Dauncey family who owned it until 1820 when it was sold to David Ricardo of Gatcombe Park, Gloucestershire. During this period of ownership there were associations with the poet William Wordsworth. Mary Wordsworth's brother, Tom Hutchinson, was the tenant and the Wordsworths were frequent visitors. William's portrait, bequeathed to the house, was hung in the Great Hall. The north and south ranges were the first to be built; the south range contains the Great Hall, originally a banqueting hall that was built in 1340 with a roof that has cambered tie beams and king posts. It has a massive stone fireplace and a stone staircase leading down into the courtyard. The drawing room was built at the end of the 17th century and the library, formerly the Elizabethan solar, has a plaster relief ceiling and wood panelling of a later period. The Queen Anne parlour, built in the 18th century, has an oval plaster ceiling. There is a medieval moat surrounding the house crossed by two bridges to the north and south. In 1913 the Astley family restored the house and started to extend the old building adding the east wing in 1915. Inside there is a wealth of exposed, oak timber framing. The house, which is a listed Grade 1 building, and its estate of woods and farmland that extends to 531 acres was recently advertised for sale at £3.5 million.

BRINSOP COURT

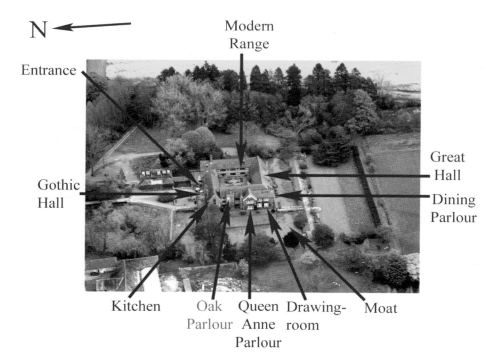

N ←

Modern Range

Entrance

Gothic Hall

Great Hall

Dining Parlour

Kitchen · Oak Parlour · Queen Anne Parlour · Drawing-room · Moat

MOCCAS

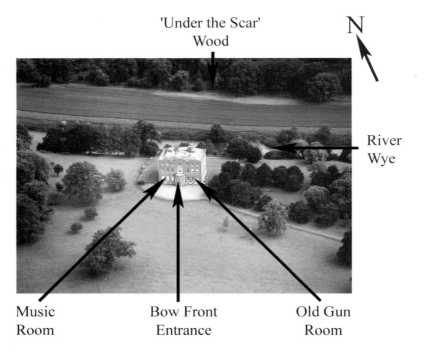

'Under the Scar' Wood

N

River Wye

Music Room — Bow Front Entrance — Old Gun Room

Moccas Court stands on a bank above the River Wye and is approached by a drive through the park from the B4352 Bredwardine to Madley road. The name Moccas is Welsh and means *swine moor*. The grounds were landscaped by Capability Brown in 1778 and added to by Humphrey Repton in 1803. This picture is of the south face of the court, which was built by Anthony Keck to plans by Robert Adam. The curved entrance porch embellishes the rather plain south front, while inside are a fine oval staircase and a circular room with its early and rare wallpaper. The architect John Nash probably designed the entrance lodges. In 1946 Sir William Cornewall, who was unmarried, sold the furniture and contents owned by his family for many generations and eventually the Chestermaster family inherited the estate, which is now open on certain days during the summer. Nearby is the medieval Fallow Deer Park of 300 acres, which is one of the very few left in the county when at one time there were thirty-five. The distant woods lie under *the Scar*, which is a rocky outcrop on the north bank of the river and just off the picture to the left.

The name Hay-on-Wye [Y-Gelli in Welsh] means *a fenced or hedged enclosure.* Since Norman times, for administration purposes, it has been divided into English Hay and Welsh Hay. Today the town is mostly in Wales but the smaller eastern section is Herefordshire. This photograph was taken from over Wales looking towards Herefordshire. The Welsh and County boundary runs along the Dulas Brook and at its confluence with the river Wye, continues north-eastwards along the middle of the river. The town is situated to the north east of the Brecon Beacons National Park, 19 miles west of Hereford and in its centre is the 12th century Norman Castle with a fire damaged house, which is now the home of Richard Booth, the instigator of the town's famous bookshops. He started his business in 1962 and has made the town world famous for its thirty-two second-hand bookshops. The horse drawn tramway from Brecon to Kington was opened on the 14th May 1816 and was used to bring coal from the canal wharf at Brecon to Hay. In 1862 the line was sold to the developers of the steam railway and rebuilt with a railway station at the east end of the town, which closed in 1962. This is now an industrial and retail estate. The present river bridge, built in 1957, has 6 pre-stressed concrete spans. This replaced an iron bridge built in 1868 which crossed not only the river but also the railway line. The first bridge of stone, built in 1763, was a toll bridge, which took tolls until 1933. Both Offa's Dyke Footpath and the Wye Valley Walk cross the bridge. Clyro village, just 3/4 mile away was home to the famous Victorian vicar and diarist Francis Kilvert

HAY ON WYE

N

B4350 to Clifford

Old Railway Station Trading Estate

River Wye

B4351 Road Bridge to Clyro

Dulas Brook

Hay Castle

St. Mary's Church

Clock Tower

Tourist Information

The privately owned bridge at Whitney-on-Wye, which lies about 15 miles west of Hereford, is the last remaining toll bridge in the county. It is the fourth bridge to be built on this site, with three timber spans and two semicircular stone arches, covering a length of 40 metres. Over the years the river has changed its course; the first bridge on this site was built in 1774, which was replaced by another three bridges in quick succession as the first two were washed away. The last of these was erected in 1782 and two of its stone arches remain under the present bridge. There is a toll of 50p for vehicles and no charge to pedestrians. The income is tax-free but the owners have to maintain the bridge, a grade 2 listed structure. In 1818 the horse drawn railway from Hay to Kington was opened and because of exclusive crossing rights the tramway was obliged to lay its track across the toll bridge. It was not until 1863 that the Hereford, Hay and Brecon Railway obtained the right to replace the tramway and build a new railway bridge 150 yards upstream but they had to guarantee to pay the tolls on the old bridge of up to £345 a year, a situation which continued until the closure of the railway at the end of 1962. Francis Kilvert wrote in his diary on 11th November 1878 - *the Whitney iron railway bridge was carried away last night by flood and two miles of line seriously damaged.* When the line closed in 1962 the bridge was dismantled. The course of the old railway track can be seen on the photograph.

WHITNEY ON WYE

River Wye

Boat Inn

Old Railway Line

Rhydpool

Witney Toll Bridge

Old Railway Line

B4350 Road to Hay on Wye

N

The name Weobley means *Wibba's clearing*. This famous black and white village has an example of almost every type of timber framing from the 14th to 17th centuries. The old castle built by Roger de Lacy was the site of several bloody battles. An early engraving shows that it was a rectangular keep with six round towers and a gateway on the north side. The Parish Church of St. Peter and Paul on the north side of the village marks the earliest settlement as records show that it had a priest as early as 1086. The present church, although it has traces of Norman work, was built during the 13th century and the tower in the 14th century. The tower has 6 bells, the earliest dated 1605. Inside the church is a memorial to Col. John Birch who took Hereford during the Civil War and was later Member of Parliament for Weobley. It was Roger de Lacy who laid out a borough between his new castle and the church, which grew as a market centre and became the village we know today. Weobley was once famous for its beer that was sold across the local area as far as the Welsh border. The author Mary Ellen Leather, who wrote The Folklore of Herefordshire, first published in 1912, lived here.

WEOBLEY

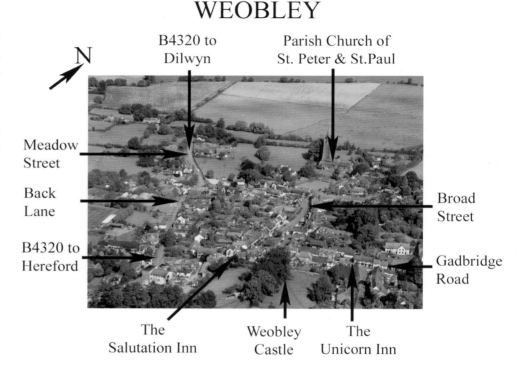

N

B4320 to Dilwyn

Parish Church of St. Peter & St.Paul

Meadow Street

Back Lane

B4320 to Hereford

Broad Street

Gadbridge Road

The Salutation Inn

Weobley Castle

The Unicorn Inn

The name Dinmore comes from the Welsh *din-mawr*, *great hill*. A settlement was founded here when the Knights of Saint John of Jerusalem built a preceptory. They were originally based in Jerusalem but when that fell they moved to the port of Acre, then to Cyprus, from there to Rhodes for 200 years and finally to Malta. In Herefordshire their prime possession was Dinmore Manor. They also owned property that included a chapel in Marden [demolished in the 20th century] and a hospital in Widemarsh Street, Hereford, where they offered shelter and refreshments to travellers. In 1310, on the suppression of the Order of the Templars, the Order of the Hospitallers was endowed with their possessions. The chapel, dedicated to St John the Evangelist, the patron saint of travellers, was built between the 12th and 14th centuries with an oak roof. On the outside wall there are two early sundials. The pipe organ came from Moccas Court Herefordshire.

The earliest part of the house dates from the late 16th century; inside there is still a Jacobean mantelpiece and panelling of the same period. Richard Hollins Murray, inventor of the reflective cats eyes on our roads, who extended the old house by building a music room 67 feet long, 25 feet wide and 25 feet high and cloisters using stone from the Old Gaol in Commercial Road, Hereford, purchased the house in 1927. The roof is a medieval hammer beam replica with carvings. The architect was Bettington from Hereford. The west wall of the cloisters is closed and the eight tracery windows are glazed with beautiful stained glass. On the south wall the window depicts scenes from the life of a knight during the crusades. There is a small dovecote on the octagonal tower. The gardens in front of the house and cloisters are beautifully landscaped with a spectacular view to the east as far as the Malvern Hills. The house has recently been sold.

DINMORE MANOR

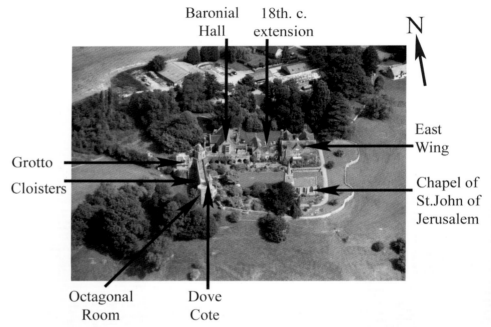

Baronial Hall

18th. c. extension

N

Grotto

Cloisters

East Wing

Chapel of St.John of Jerusalem

Octagonal Room

Dove Cote

BODENHAM VILLAGE

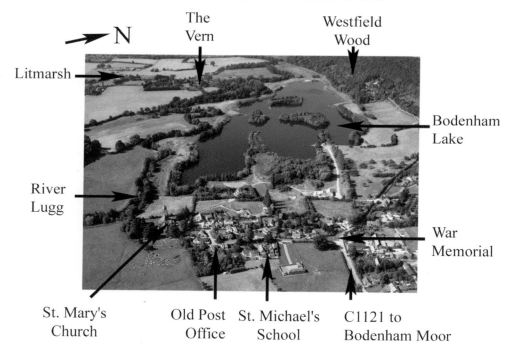

The name Bodenham means *Boda's water meadow*, which is very appropriate since the old sand and gravel pits are now landscaped with lakes and islands. Now owned by Herefordshire Council, this site has a wealth of wildlife, which attracts many naturalists from far and wide. The Church of St. Michael was built in the 13th and 14th centuries. Nicholas Pevsner describes the tower that has six bells as *finished with the funny but memorable feature of a little pyramid roof set on top of a never completed recessed spire*. The meandering lines of trees near the Church mark the course of the River Lugg, which was said to divide the village with a social boundary, the collar and tie workers living to the west. The road bridge over the River Lugg is just off the picture along the C1121 to Bodenham Moor. At the nearby road junction are the War Memorial and remains of the Market Cross, possibly from the 14th century that has only the stump of the shaft left.

BODENHAM MOOR

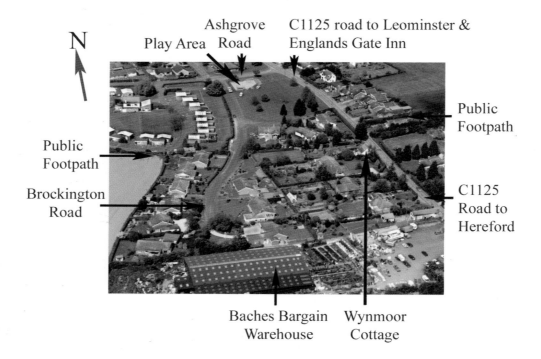

Bodenham Moor lies 7 miles north of Hereford on the C1125 road. It is about 1/2 mile long and is surrounded by modern houses on several small estates to the north around Brockington Road and Orchard Close in the south. Between these is a large warehouse store, Baches Bargains, founded in 1980 in a farm building and now retailing a diverse variety of items. To the north is The England's Gate Inn that has new owners who have brought it back to life after several years of decline and limited opening.

Hampton Court stands on a bank beside the River Lugg on the north side of Dinmore Hill between Hereford and Leominster on the A417 road. The impressive house dates from 1434, built by Sir Rowland Lenthall who was granted a licence to crenellate it. The present building is probably on the original layout of four ranges round a courtyard with the gatehouse and walls of the chapel the oldest remaining parts. The building was extensively re-modelled by Lord Conningsby about 1700. R. Arkwright [one of the cotton spinner's family] purchased the estate in 1817 and introduced a complex system of water channels, ducts and water driven equipment, which have recently been re-created and restored. The gardens have been landscaped over the centuries by several well-known names including Humphrey Repton who planned the parkland in front of the house in the 1790's. There used to be a deer park on Dinmore Hill where some deer can still be seen. The house had several owners during the 20th century and was eventually purchased by the Van-Kampen family from Lake Michigan U.S.A, who have invested a lot of money on its restoration. It is now in superb order with kitchens to match any top-class hotel. Dorrell and Wheeler have designed the landscaped gardens, using different period styles and creating a maze with a central tower that has an exit tunnel. The gardens were opened on June 24th 2000 with a concert and spectacular firework display and are now open to the public during the summer months.

HAMPTON COURT

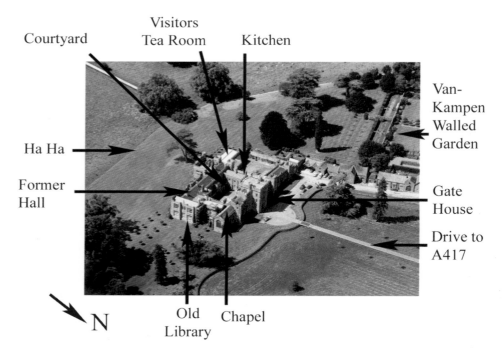

Courtyard · Visitors Tea Room · Kitchen · Van-Kampen Walled Garden · Ha Ha · Former Hall · Gate House · Drive to A417 · N · Old Library · Chapel

DINMORE RAILWAY TUNNEL

N ↑

Rose Cottage Garden

C1121 Road to Bodenham

Trickland Coppice

Station House

C1121 Road to A49 & Burghope

Railway Inn

Dinmore Railway Tunnel is on the Shrewsbury to Hereford railway line, which was sanctioned by Parliament in 1846 for a single line. It took four years to raise the money to employ the contractor Thomas Brassey, to not only build the line but for him to have enough confidence in its prospects to offer to work the line at his own expense. The single line was completed in stages, finishing in Hereford. It opened for goods' trucks on 30th July 1852 and all traffic on 6th December 1853. The Dinmore tunnel, 1060 yards long, was part of the last section built and was opened at a ceremony on 16th September 1853 when the last of 3 1/4 million bricks were laid. The entrance has the coat of arms of the Arkwright family, from Hampton Court, Bodenham, incorporated into the stonework. In 1893 the Railway Inn was used for an inquest into the death of a navvy, Thomas Mills, who was crushed by a rock fall during blasting for a second tunnel. The C1121 road was re-aligned in 1893 to make space for a waiting room on the 'up line' [on the left side] to Shrewsbury when the second tunnel came into use. Note that the 'up line' is at a slightly higher level than the 'down line'

MARLBROOK

Crumb Storage Silos

Crumb Production Block

Sugar Silos

A49 to Leominster

N

Lagoon Nature Reserve

Boiler House

Cadbury's Reception

Hereford to Shrewsbury Railway

A49 to Hereford

Cadburys, the famous chocolate manufacturer, opened its factory at Marlbrook, 2 miles south of Leominster on the A49 road, in 1936. This factory does not make the finished chocolate but the milk crumb. Marlbrook was chosen because of its location in the heart of the country's milk supply. For example in 1950 they took supplies from over 1,300 local farms, a high proportion of deliveries being in churns. With the gradual closure of crumb making facilities in other factories between 1965 and 1982 Marlbrook as-sumed full responsibility for supplying the whole of Cadbury's Ltd. As the demand for milk chocolate grew the factory expanded and is now in use 24 hours a day. There are eleven plants operating, the last came on stream in 1995. In 1997 Marlbrook employed eighty-five people and had a daily intake of 500,000 litres of milk from which enough crumb was made to make the equivalent of 1.5 million 200g bars of Cadbury's Dairy Milk Chocolate.

BROMYARD

N

Parish Church of St. Peter

Station Industrial Estate [Hydro Automotive Structures]

Church Street

Broad Street

Sherford Street

High Street

Blacksmiths Court

A44 Worcester Road

A44 to Leominster

Bromyard By-Pass

The Falcon Hotel

Stonehill Drive

Bromyard, meaning *enclosure in the broom* is a market town, which stands high above the River Frome. The old railway station site, once the terminus of the Bromyard and Linton light railway, is now an industrial estate. The parish church of St. Peter is situated in a high position. It has a Saxon foundation but was rebuilt and extended into a cruciform shape during the 12th century. The bell tower has a distinctive turret corner, which contains a spiral staircase. The church now owns the town's ancient bushel measure inscribed 'by act of Parliament 1670'. The Tourist Information Centre is nearby in Rowberry Street. All along Broad Street and High Street are long narrow plots of land called *burgages*.

The parish church of St. Michael and All Angels, which was built partly in the 12th century but mainly in the 13th stands over a deserted medieval village. There are a few scattered houses nearby but the centre of the village moved about 1/2 mile to the southwest sometime after the Black Death. The north transept still retains its 14th century roof but the church tower was rebuilt in 1822. Just to the east of the church, hidden by the trees, is the castle that consists of a motte about 50 yards in diameter, with the remains of a stone keep and bailey surrounded with a wet moat. The castle was probably established shortly after the Norman Conquest as it was mentioned in 1209 and according to a contract of 1391 between the stone mason and Sir John Devereux it had a stone hall 44 feet long and 26 wide with four doors and three windows. In front of the churchyard wall there was a horse drawn tramway, which ran from Brecon via Hay on Wye to Kington. This opened on May 1st 1820 and carried coal from the canal wharf at Brecon, and unloaded at a tramway wharf opposite the church, now the entrance to Lynhales. Lime was made at the Dolyhir Quarry near Kington and taken to the canal. In 1862 the tram-road shareholders decided to sell to the proposed steam railway which ran from Hay to Kington. According to an 1875 steam railway timetable, the journey from Kington to Lyonshall took ten minutes.

LYONSHALL CHURCH

N

Vicarage

St. Michael's
Church

Old
Castle

Course of
Old Hay to
Kington
Tramway

A44 to
Kington

The
Laurels

A44 to
Pembridge

Public Footpath & Drive
to Lyn Hales

Old Weymouth
Arms

Old School

Kington has retained its name from pre- Norman times and was *Chingtune* in the Domesday Book. It lies at the foot of Bradnor Hill at the confluence of the rivers Arrow and Gilwern. There was a castle on the western side above the Gilwern, facing towards the Welsh border. All that remains are traces of the rampart and a dry moat. Nearby is the church of St. Mary, which is about half a mile away from the town centre. Turnpike Gate Toll House on Bridge Street collected tolls from 1756 until 1880 when they were abolished. The nearby bridge dates from 1810, which has since been strengthened and widened. The first horse drawn railway ran from Brecon through Hay on Wye and Eardisley and was opened on May 1st 1820. The steam train arrived in Kington from Leominster on 30th June 1862. Now the site of the old railway station is an industrial estate. The straight road is Victoria Road that changes to Duke Street, High Street, then Mill Street and finally Park Avenue. Church Street leads to the old castle and church. At the junction of Church Street and High Street is the Market Hall designed by Herefordshire architect F. R. Kempson and described by Nicholas Pevsner as *ugly*. This replaced an earlier Market Hall of 1654 built by the King's carpenter John Abel. The jubilee tower was added in 1897. On the opposite side of the road are the Burton Hotel, which was built in 1851, and its Assembly Room of 1856. In High Street opposite Bridge Street, is the Old Town Hall built by Benjamin Wishlade in 1845. The Baptist Chapel in Bridge Street was built for £2,000 in 1868 and could accommodate a congregation of 600.

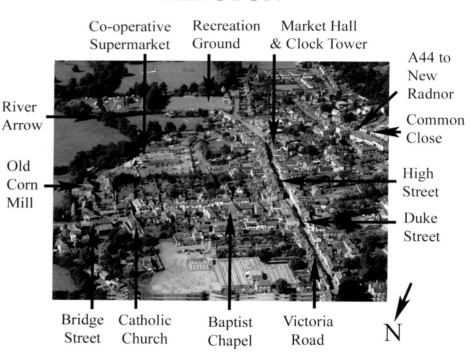

KINGTON

Co-operative Supermarket · Recreation Ground · Market Hall & Clock Tower · A44 to New Radnor · River Arrow · Common Close · Old Corn Mill · High Street · Duke Street · Bridge Street · Catholic Church · Baptist Chapel · Victoria Road · N

PEMBRIDGE

New Inn

River Arrow

A44 to Kington [West-Street]

Bridge Street

Market Hall

A44 to Eardisland

N

C1083 Road to Luntley

Castle Moat

St. Mary's Church

Pembridge, one of Herefordshire's best-known black and white villages, is situated 7 miles west of Leominster. Its name means *head of the bridge*. The parish church of St. Mary built in the 13th and 14th centuries, has a detached octagonal wood-framed bell tower built in three diminishing stages with a pyramidal roof containing 5 bells. The earliest timbers in the tower date from the 13th century. Next to the graveyard is the castle mound measuring about 25 by 35 metres and a dry moat. In the centre of the village stands the Market House with its eight carved posts, which originally had an upper storey and was possibly on a nearby site. The New Inn is a much-photographed building and has featured in many calendars. The village has several tourist attractions, including Pembridge Terracotta, who make pots using local clay, a crafts gallery in the converted chapel, antique shops and a visitor's centre.

EARDISLAND

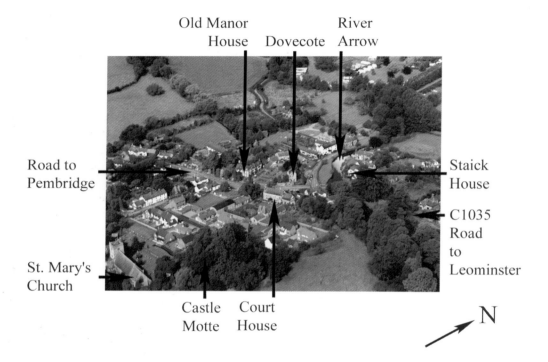

Old Manor House • Dovecote • River Arrow • Road to Pembridge • Staick House • C1035 Road to Leominster • St. Mary's Church • Castle Motte • Court House • N

The name Eardisland comes from *earl* and *lene*, an area of land between the rivers Arrow and Lugg. Being on the Black and White Village Trail it is one of the most visited villages of north Herefordshire. The river Arrow flows through the village, past the mown grass banks, flowerbeds, picturesque houses and under the road bridge. The church of St. Mary has a 13th century nave and a west tower replaced in 1728 that was further restored in 1864. Near the church, hidden among the trees is the Castle with a 16 feet high mound and moat 50 yards in diameter. There are many black and white houses.

The one near the bridge is called Staick House that was built in the 14th century with a great hall. On the other side of the river is the timber-framed two-storey manor house built in the 17th century. The dovecote is square with a roof gable on each side, a square roof lantern and weather vane. This has just been restored and is now used as a gallery. On the north side of the Old School House, that became the Reading Rooms in 1936, is the village whipping post.

KINGSLAND

Kingsland is called *Lene* in the Domesday Book, which is an ancient name for the district in which it lies. The northwestern end of North Road joins the Roman Road, Watling Street at the Monument Inn. This ancient road connects the Herefordshire Roman towns of Leintwardine and Kenchester. From here it is one mile to the parish church of St. Michael that was built in the 14th century with a roof supported by king post trusses. The remains of a motte and bailey and a castle rampart and ditches are in the field adjacent to the Churchyard. There is a public footpath across the castle earthworks to Harbour Farm. Philip de Braose is thought to have built the Castle in the early 13th century, yet there is no mention of a Castle here during the conflict between the houses of York and Lancaster at the nearby Battle of Mortimers Cross on 2nd February 1461, where 4,000 soldiers were killed and Owen Tudor taken prisoner. Along North Road are a large number of timber-framed and historic houses and at its junction with Lugg Green Road to Yarpole is the Corners Inn.

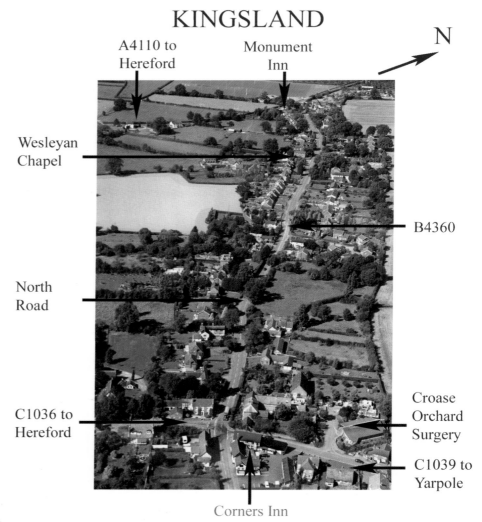

A4110 to Hereford

Monument Inn

N

Wesleyan Chapel

B4360

North Road

C1036 to Hereford

Croase Orchard Surgery

C1039 to Yarpole

Corners Inn

CROFT CASTLE

Dining Room — Courtyard

Oak Room

St.Michael's Church

Blue Room — Drawing Room — Library

N

The imposing rectangular shape of Croft Castle dominates the small church of Saint Michael which was built in the 13th century and has a 17th century bell turret. Inside there are box pews, a west gallery and a fine monument of 1509 dedicated to Sir Richard Croft, who fought at the battle of nearby Mortimers Cross in 1461, and his wife. Outside, just a few yards to the west, is the castle that was mentioned in the Domesday Book as the manor of Bernard de Croft whose descendants kept it until it was sold to the Knight family of Downton Castle [page 124] in 1746. It was bought back by the Croft family in 1923, who still have apartments there, even though the National Trust now owns it. The first Baron Croft, created in 1671, was a Dean and later Bishop of Her-

eford. On the death of the 12th Baron, the estate of 1,375 acres was saved by the land fund. The approach road to the Castle is lined with an avenue of ancient oaks and beeches. The grounds were landscaped in the late 18th century based on the ideas of Uvedale Price of Foxley and Richard Payne Knight of Downton Castle, neighbouring Herefordshire squires who supported the picturesque movement. Much of the castle and external turrets date from the 15th to early 18th century. The furnished rooms are open to visitors during the summer months. Behind the house is the well-manicured walled garden that contains many rare varieties of apple trees, shrubs, roses and plants.

STAUNTON ON ARROW

Grove Wood · Grove Farm · Mowley Wood · Horseway Head · Castle Mound · River Arrow · St.Peter's Church · Old Vicarage · C1203 to Stockley Cross · N

The name Staunton on Arrow means *settlement on stony ground near the River Arrow.* The parish church of St. Peters, a Victorian building that dominates the village, was designed and constructed by the architect Thomas Nicholson in 1856. It is a large church for such a small village. Nearby is a circular castle motte about 20 yards across and about 26 feet above the surrounding dry ditch. The church was apparently built on a castle bailey and there are other enclosures to the south and west. The Roman road from Mortimer's Cross to Clyro, crossed the river Arrow by a ford near the bridge. There is an Iron Age hill fort on Wapley Hill about 2 miles north west of the village that covers an area of 25 acres and has a well, which never runs dry.

It is thought that the name Leominster is derived from the Old English Lene *floods and streams,* the name of the district on the Rivers Lugg and Arrow. John Abel built the old Town Hall now called The Grange which was erected as a Butter Cross and Sessions Chamber in 1633. It originally stood at the junction of Broad Street and High Street then was sold to the Arkwrights of Hampton Court, Bodenham who re-erected it on the present site as a house. The Priory Church of St. Peter and St. Paul is a short distance from the town centre. The River Lugg was made navigable in 1714 down-stream to the river Wye at Mordiford. The Pinsley Brook and Kenwater run behind the Fire Station. In the middle of the photograph is the commercial centre of Leominster with its picturesque Drapers Lane and its neighbour High Street. There are numerous antique and interesting privately owned shops to browse in, a welcome change to the usual multiple chain shops found in most towns and cities.

LEOMINSTER

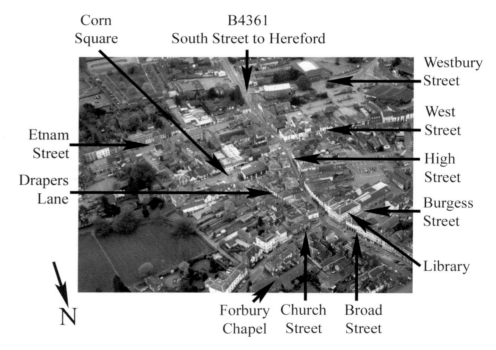

The Priory Church of St. Peter and St. Paul, in the centre of the photograph is surrounded by its churchyard and green. It was originally a monastry from about the 9th century to its dissolution in 1046. Henry I donated it to Reading Abbey in 1123 as a Benedictine cell or priory. The earliest surviving part of the Church is the north nave and aisle, next to the tower. The central nave was added in the 13th century and the south aisle in the 14th. The interior is very large, about 125 feet long by 124 feet wide, built in the Norman, Early English, Decorated and Perpendicular styles. The Priory contains some of the best sculpture of the Herefordshire School. An ancient 12-yard long "Ducking Stool", last used in 1813, can be seen inside the church.

Behind the church are the Priory House and Herefordshire Council Offices, which stands in the site of the Saxon Monastery. The Forbury Chapel on Church Street was founded in 1292 by John Peckham [Archbishop of Canterbury] as the chapel of St. Thomas of Canterbury and has a hammer beam roof, 64 feet long and 32 feet wide, erected in the 15th century. Its position was such that it was partly in the town and partly in the Priory Precinct. The most recent building in the area is the Community Centre.

LEOMINSTER
PRIORY

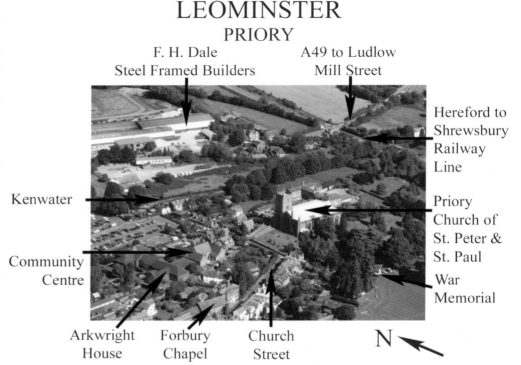

F. H. Dale
Steel Framed Builders

A49 to Ludlow
Mill Street

Hereford to Shrewsbury Railway Line

Kenwater

Priory Church of St. Peter & St. Paul

Community Centre

War Memorial

Arkwright House

Forbury Chapel

Church Street

N

BERRINGTON HALL

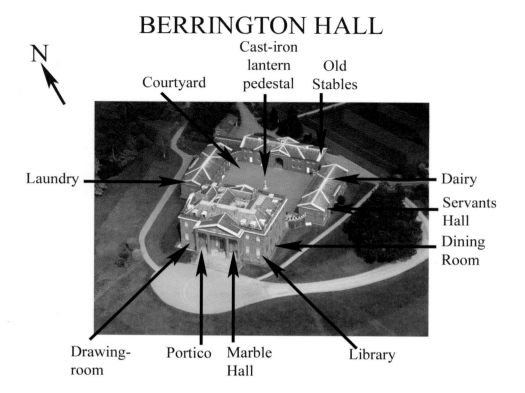

N

Cast-iron
lantern
pedestal

Courtyard

Old
Stables

Laundry

Dairy

Servants
Hall

Dining
Room

Drawing-
room

Portico

Marble
Hall

Library

Berrington meaning *settlement by the burgh/stronghold* is adjacent to the A49 Ludlow to Leominster road, 2 1/2 miles north of Leominster. The original owners of the estate were the Cornewall family from Moccas. It was later sold to Thomas Harley of Brampton Bryan who made his fortune as a banker and Government contractor. In 1778 he started to landscape the grounds on 'Capability' Brown's concepts and built the present house to Henry Holland's plans. The design of the house was made up of three pavilions attached to each other. The house was inherited by the female line and passed into the Rodney family of naval fame. In 1901 the 7th Lord Rodney died and the estate was sold to Fredrick Cawley who later became Lord Cawley. When he died in 1957 the estate was passed to the National Trust in lieu of death duties. The original stables were destroyed by fire. The house is furnished with most of the family furniture and possessions with additions from the Elmar Digby collection presented to the National Trust. The last member of the family to live in the house was Lady Cawley who died in 1978 at Berrington just after celebrating her 100th birthday. The house is closed during the winter.

GATLEY PARK

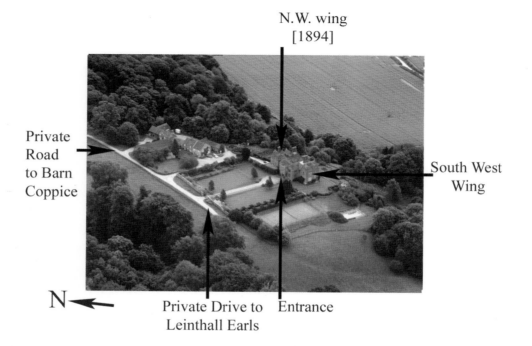

N.W. wing
[1894]

Private
Road
to Barn
Coppice

South West
Wing

N ←

Private Drive to   Entrance
Leinthall Earls

The name Gatley means *pass through a clearing or* geat. Gatley Park is a fairly large house at the end of a long drive that starts in Leinthall Earls and ends on the side of a valley opposite Oaker Wood. The Dunne family, who own the Park, purchased it in 1673. According to the Victorian book *Mansions and Manors of Herefordshire* Gatley was at one time used as a stud for breeding mares and excellent horses. The earliest part of the house was a timber framed, square-shaped hunting lodge of the 1630's, which was extended in 1894 and again more recently. Inside are some early features including the staircase and hall that extends across the whole of the original house. In recent years members of the Royal family have visited the house.

The name Wigmore means *moor of Wiga*. The Roman road - Watling Street passes to the east where there are the remains of a Roman camp in a nearby field belonging to Bury Court. The Domesday Book records that Ralph de Mortimer held the small castle that stood west of the church. The parish church of St. James is almost hidden but stands on high ground to the west of the A4110 Hereford to Leintwardine road. The church has a Norman nave with a herringbone masonry pattern on the outside of the north wall. At the top edge of the picture is another, larger 12th century castle on a hilltop, which was greatly extended in the 14th century by the Mortimers [page 120]. The old buildings at Bury Court have been renovated and several houses built nearby. The local schools, Wigmore High School and the nearby Primary School, are visible with their playing fields as well as the Compasses Hotel and its nearby Mobile Home Park. There are several small businesses in the village including a Post Office, general stores, garage and a specialist musical instrument and furniture maker, Mr. Ellis. A local heritage leaflet, *The Wigmore History Trail* by Jim Tonkin, lists 53 buildings of varying degrees of importance and is available free of charge in the stores next to the garage.

WIGMORE

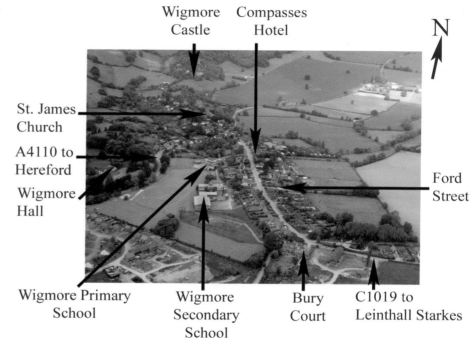

Wigmore Castle

Compasses Hotel

N

St. James Church

A4110 to Hereford

Wigmore Hall

Ford Street

Wigmore Primary School

Wigmore Secondary School

Bury Court

C1019 to Leinthall Starkes

WIGMORE CASTLE

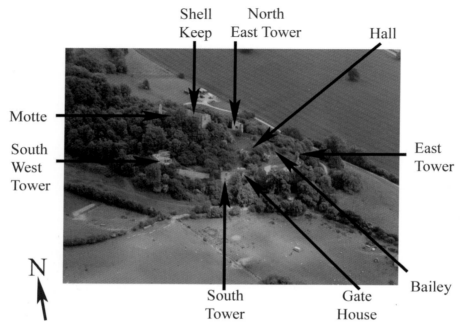

Motte · Shell Keep · North East Tower · Hall · East Tower · South West Tower · South Tower · Gate House · Bailey · N

Wigmore Castle, which is visible from the road, stands on a knoll a few hundred yards to the north of the village. This photograph was taken toward the end of a million pound conservation programme undertaken by English Heritage in 1999, and there is still some scaffolding visible on the southwest tower. Turf from the top of the ruined walls was carefully removed and returned after restoration. This type of conservation is a new idea that should ensure a long future for the castle ruins. The first recorded castle was built in 1086 by William FitzOsbern, then was later possessed by Ralph de Mortimer and remained in his family until the 15th century. The walls and towers were built in the 13th and early 14th century and surround the inner bailey. It was from here that Edward Duke of York advanced on the 3rd February 1461 to the battle of Mortimer's Cross, where he was the victor and became King Edward IV. For many centuries it was an important fortress but was dismantled during the Civil War and has been a ruin ever since. It is open to visitors but they are requested to park in the village as directed, while the disabled are advised that it is unwise to attempt the climb. At present there are no information leaflets or books about the castle available in the village.

The name Brampton Bryan originates from *settlement by the broom now owned by Brian.* Brian de Brampton was the Lord of the Manor in 1185. The village green is in the centre of the village, which has a Post Office, shop and a farriery. In the middle of the picture is Brampton Bryan Hall which is owned by the Harley family who are said to be the junior family of the Harleys, Earls of Oxford and Mortimer. The house though still large, is a much-reduced version of an earlier building. The entrance porch on the west front, hidden from the camera, has Roman Doric columns. In the drawing room is a remarkable Victorian fireplace of white marble from Eywood House, which was owned by the Oxford family but demolished in 1954. The estate has one of the few deer parks left in the county. Just a few yards away from the house are the ruins of a castle that was known to have existed in 1295, was extended in1309 but almost completely destroyed during the Civil war. It was besieged by the Royalists' in 1643 and taken during another raid in 1644. The twin towers nearest the camera are the 14th century entrance and gatehouse. The distant ruins were part of the Great Hall. In the foreground is the Parish Church of St. Barnabas that was almost totally destroyed during the Civil War by the Royalists but rebuilt in 1656 by Sir Robert Harley. It forms a large rectangular shape and has an impressive high double hammer beam roof. Note the attractive Walnut Tree cottage in the foreground.

BRAMPTON BRYAN

N

Brampton Bryan Hall

Castle Great Hall

Brampton Bryan Castle entrance

St.Barnabas Church

C1001 to Bucknell

C1001 to Village Centre

Walnut Tree Cottage

Church Road

DOWNTON CASTLE

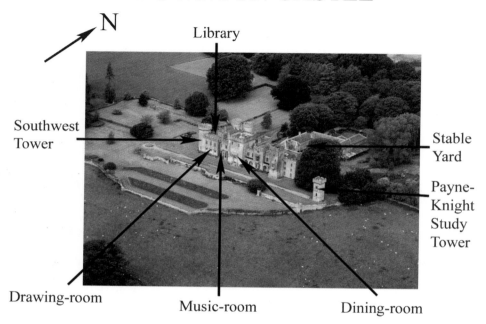

N

Library

Southwest Tower

Stable Yard

Payne-Knight Study Tower

Drawing-room

Music-room

Dining-room

Downton Castle is set high on a bank above the River Teme in a most attractive wooded gorge. Downton village is at the entrance to the gorge. The old Ludlow to Leintwardine road used to pass through the village but was diverted to avoid the landscaped castle grounds. The castle, built by Richard Payne Knight, grandson of Richard Knight of Madeley, one of the early Shropshire ironmasters who bought the estate, looks weathered and a lot older than it is. R. P. Knight was an archaeologist, anthropologist, prolific writer and poet. The castle, designed by Payne Knight, using only the minimal services of an architect, was completed by 1778 and is one of the earliest contrived castellated castles. There were major additions and changes during the years 1860-1870 when an entrance tower, chapel and music room were added. Pevsner describes the interior as of beautiful classical proportions with the principal room an imitation of the Pantheon in Rome i.e. circular and domed with a central eye, in the largest of the south towers. The castle grounds, also designed by Richard Payne Knight who was an exponent of the picturesque in landscaping are an important feature. He was the author of a book, *The Landscape,* in which he attacked 'Capability' Brown's mild and gentle layouts and pleaded for an appreciation of wild nature only doing a little planting and cutting of paths to his follies.

Leintwardine, meaning *the homestead by the fast flowing river,* is adjacent to the confluence of the rivers Teme and Clun on the A4110 road, which leads south to Wigmore and Hereford. The village is one of the oldest settlements in the county being on the site of the Roman Legionary Fort of Bravinium on Watling Street. This road went north to the Roman town of Wroxeter near Shrewsbury and south to Caerleon near Newport. Roman Watling Street, now called High Street ran through Leintwardine, while the present day named Watling Street was outside the Roman town. The photograph shows the rectangular Roman town layout now made up of garden hedges and roads. The Roman baths were discovered under the village garage during past excavations which over the last one hundred and fifty years have provided a wealth of Roman items, but the detailed layout of the town is unknown. Most of the village has been built outside the Roman Town. The parish church of St. Mary Magdalene was built mainly in the 13th and 14th centuries with the chancel over the Roman defensive ramparts and higher than the nave. There was never a border castle here, the nearest being at Brampton Bryan.

LEINTWARDINE

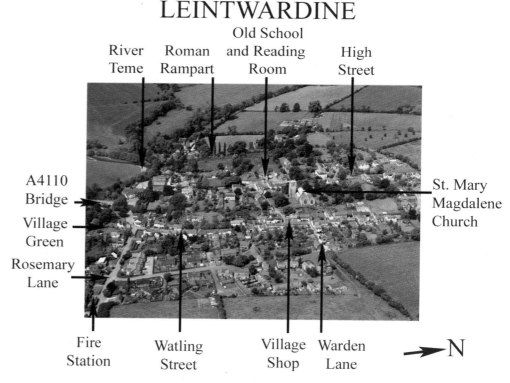

River Teme · Roman Rampart · Old School and Reading Room · High Street · St. Mary Magdalene Church · A4110 Bridge · Village Green · Rosemary Lane · Fire Station · Watling Street · Village Shop · Warden Lane · N

INDEX